CONTENTS

CHAPTER 1 | THE GATE OF THE HELL

"The Gate of the Hell" is a song by JAM Project feat. Fukuyama Yoshiki, the second OVA OP for Mazinkaizer.

WILL BE AN AV.

SO, MISORA...

YOUR NEXT JOB...

Sanada Hikaru
PRESIDENT OF SPACE WOLF ENTERTAINMENT PRODUCTIONS.

HEAR ME?

I'LL SPEAK UP.

I SAID AN AV.

I'M SORRY?

SUPERIOR.

EXQUISITE!

CLAP パチ
パチ
パチ CLAP
CLAP

I THOUGHT, IT'S GOT TO BE HER!

I SAW YOUR DVD.

I WAS RIGHT!

HA

HA HA!

YOU RARELY SEE IT EXECUTED SO PERFECTLY!

THIS IS THE VERY ESSENCE OF SHURI-TE*-- NAIFANCHI!

AV Director Victor Iba

*Shuri-te refers to all Okinawan martial arts, including karate, grappling, and weapon arts.

DID YOU READ THE SCRIPT?

WELL?!

YOUR LINE IS SIR, YES, SIR!

OKAY ...

AH HA HA...

BY DOING IT RIGHT!

PROVE IT!

I READ THE SCRIPT!

SIR, YES, SIR! I READ THE SCRIPT!

THE ALL-IDOL BLACK BELT HUNDRED-MAN OPEN! IF SHE LOSES, SHE GETS GANG-BANGED BY A HUNDRE MEN!

BAM

THE MOMENT YOU FAIL, THE NIGHTMARISH LEGAL RAPE BEGINS!!

THEY'LL ATTACK, AND ATTEMPT TO MAKE YOU SUBMIT!!

AN ARMY OF BUKKAKE SPECIALISTS, EAGER FOR A STRONG WOMAN...

I--

I'LL DO IT!

OMG ...

DO IT!!

MM-HMM!

YOU SHALL USE YOUR MUSCULATURE TO PUMMEL THIRSTY PERVERTS...

UNTIL, EXHAUSTED, YOU BECOME A LIVE SACRIFICE. A MODERN AMAZON!!

WA HA HA HA!

NGGGGH!

C-CURSE IT!

CURSE THE SUNLIGHT OF THE SOUTHERN ISLAND AND MY HEALTHY BEAUTY!!

IF YOU RUN INTO TROUBLE, WE'LL CUT.

HEY-- IT'S JUST A JOB. THEY'RE ACTORS, TOO!

I MEAN... I HAVE TO.

I CAN DO THIS!

HEY, THANKS.

PUT ON YOUR GI.

IT IS TIME.

CHAPTER 2 | IT'S A-A-AMAZON!

Amazon da-da-da! *is a reference to the ED of* Kamen Rider Amazon.

A HUNDRED-MAN KUMITE.

THE MOST BRUTAL TRIAL IN THE WORLD. OF KARATE!

FIGHTING ONE HUNDRED MEN IN SUCCESSION!

INTERNAL BLEEDING.

DEHYDRATION.

ARE LEFT BATTERED AND BROKEN.

THOSE WHO DO FINISH...

LIVER DAMAGE.

KIDNEY FAILURE.

CAN FAIL.

THEY SAY EVEN WORLD CHAMPIONS...

THE LINE WAS AS CLEAR AS IF IT WAS IN A MANGA.

THE DANGER ZONE.

I SAW IT CLEARLY.

AND IF YOU CROSSED IT, YOU WERE DEAD.

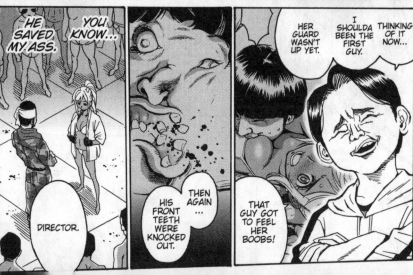

HE SAVED MY ASS.

YOU KNOW...

DIRECTOR.

THEN AGAIN...

HIS FRONT TEETH WERE KNOCKED OUT.

THINKING OF IT NOW...

I SHOULDA BEEN THE FIRST GUY.

HER GUARD WASN'T UP YET.

THAT GUY GOT TO FEEL HER BOOBS!

I WRESTLED IN COLLEGE. I WAS AN OLYMPIC HOPEFUL...

BUT A HERNIA KILLED MY DREAM.

I'M AN ACTOR/MODEL WITH EXOTIC LOOKS AND A BIG COCK.

BEGINS! HAJIME! THE FIGHT...

AH...OH YEAH.

SWAY

IT WAS DURING A BOUT OF **NIGHT-TIME WRESTLING.** ♥

IN TRAINING OR A MATCH.

I DIDN'T HURT MY BACK...

THIS SCENE IS REALLY GETTING A RISE OUT OF...

A BLACK-BELT BIMBO, HUH?

LEGIT.

RISE

RISE

MY BRAZILIAN PYTHON.

T-CK

CR--

CRUDE...

STRAIN

STRAIN

SO... HOW TO BEGIN?

I DUNNO WHAT'S NORMAL.

IS THAT... BIG?

"AND IT SHRANK!"

"BEFORE MY EYES, HE PUSHED IN ON IT..."

WHAT A MATCH!

HE'S GOT A LONG REACH.

SHE PACKS A HELLISH PUNCH.

GULP

BUT HE'S STRONG!

HE'S CRUDE...

THIS GUY...

TH--

WHO WILL WIN?!

ドクン ドクン
BADUM BADUM

SCARY AS HELL!

BADUM

TH-THIS IS...

BADUM BADUM

BADUM BADUM

THAT FLYING RIGHT AT ME.

ONE WRONG MOVE, AND IT'S OVER.

CONCUSSION...

BROKEN BONES...

MEANS...

ONE HIT...

BLOOD...

AFTER-EFFECTS...?

SERIOUSLY...

I'M FREAKING MY SHIT.

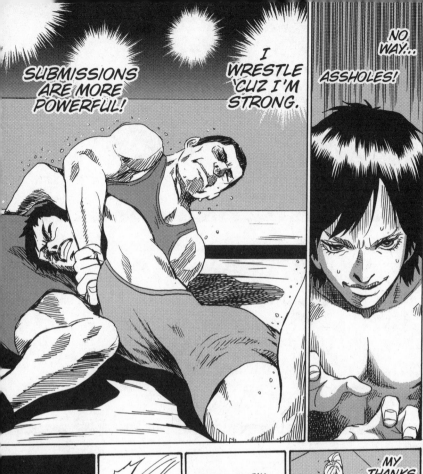

SUBMISSIONS ARE MORE POWERFUL!

I WRESTLE 'CUZ I'M STRONG.

NO WAY...

ASSHOLES!

PROVE MYSELF!

TUP

BUT TODAY...

I'M PAST MY PRIME...

I'M GONNA...

MY THANKS TO YOU...

BLACK-BELT BIMBO.

KSHH

KSHH

KSHH

SLAM

SILENCE

HANYA
NYA
FUNYA...

HUH?

CHAPTER 3 | SINGING QUEEN

"Singing Queen" is an insert song from the 1990s anime Idol Angel Youkoso Youk

WHAT KIND OF SHOW WILL SHE PUT ON NOW?!

EARNING HER THE NICK-NAME IRON WOMAN!

SHE APPEARED IN OVER A HUNDRED FILMS HER FIRST YEAR...

AH... URK...

I'M SORRY...

I SAW WHAT YOU DID TO THOSE GUYS.

DON'T GIVE ME THAT SHIT ABOUT KICKING.

I MEAN...

DON'T APOLO-GIZE.

OH, IT'S FINE, IT'S FINE.

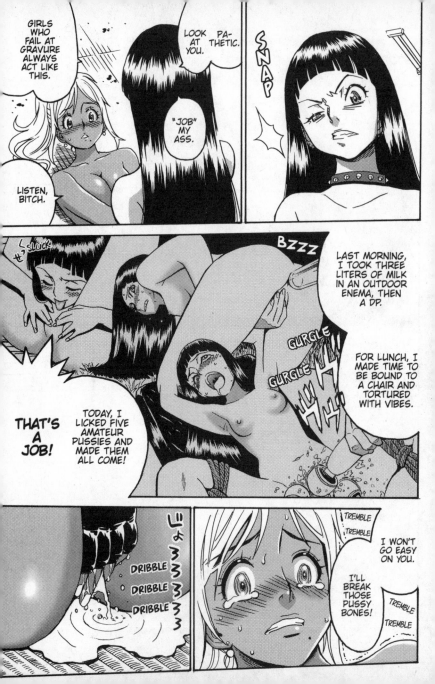

WILL YOU FIGHT?!

OR LOSE IT ALL?!

WHAT'S YOUR NEXT MOVE?!

BADUM

...

You must never let it go...

Tii...

Misora ...

Keep on training.

is the soul of us shiman-chu.*

*"Tii" is Okinawan for the hand, and is a metonym for karate.
"Shimanchu" means "islanders," the Okinawan people.

They could take our weapons...

but we always had our *tii.*

Ours is a history of struggle, whether ruled by the Chinese or persecuted by the Yamato...*

It forged our people...

like a weapon.

We don't need them.

*Yamato is an old term for the people of mainland Japan.

DAD...

Keep training...!

I'll always watch over you.

Never give up!

"Nada Sōsō", a 1998 pop song by the Okinawan band BEGIN. A popular karaoke standard.

OF TEARS!

EYES FULL...

BUT...

YEAH. WELL DONE.

YOU SHOULD KNOW...

YOU WERE GREAT.

HOW IT ENDED!

I WON FAIR AND SQUARE!

SO THAT'S...

THE TRAGIC TALE OF A SINGER WHO TRADED IN HER PITCH PIPES FOR HARD STRIKES!!

I THINK...

YOUR FUTURE LIES ELSEWHERE.

?

OH, YOU.

HAEBARU MISORA, AGE NINETEEN...

SINGING QUEEN / END

Booty
Royale

Never
Go Down
Without a
Fight!

CHAPTER 4 | CRIMSON RED

Shu-AKA- (Crimson Red) is the name of a 1998 single by Okui Masami. It's also the name of a 2003 H game.

WHAT'S WRONG?

げんなり SLUMP

YOU HAVE A NEW GIG.

I MEAN...

IT'S ANOTHER AV, RIGHT?

THEY WON'T ALWAYS BE KUMITE...

I BET THIS TIME IT'LL BE A NORMAL SCENE WITH AN ACTOR.

AGHH...

YOU'VE GOT POTEN- TIAL.

YOU'VE GOT THE WRONG IDEA.

HEY.

THAT'S PATHETIC!

I DON'T WANT MY FIRST TIME ON AN AV!

TOMOR- ROW AFTER- NOON...

SOME- ONE LIKED IT.

I SENT YOUR KUMITE FOOTAGE AROUND.

HUH!

YOU REALLY CAN BREAK ANYTHING!

WELL, TAKE A SEAT.

CRACK

WELL, IT DOESN'T MATTER EITHER WAY.

I SEE.

IT'S ALL ME!

WHAT? NO WAY!

LIKE HIDING METAL IN YOUR HANDS?

THERE'S NO TRICK TO THIS OR ANY-THING?

OH, OKAY...

"One-Week Master!"
DIRECTOR: MASAOKA EIJI

SMUSH

HAGE TRADITIONA
Premium
HAGE
ALL MALT BEER
MALT 100% HAGE BEER (DRAFT)

CRUMPLE

HUP!

I CAN CRUSH A CAN.

AGH...

IF IT'S JUST A CAN...

YOU CAN DO IT!

WHOA.

HEY.

WHAT'S THE PROBLEM?

PHEW...

THAT'S AMAZING SHIT, THOUGH.

WE CAN'T LET HER SUCCEED...

THEY'LL CUT THE FEED.

THIS'LL BE MY BIG BREAK!

A CHANCE TO SING ON TV!

KWA HA HA

IT'S LIKE HAVING DUMB-BELLS ON YOUR CHEST TWENTY-FOUR SEVEN.

SIX KILO-GRAMS OF TIT.

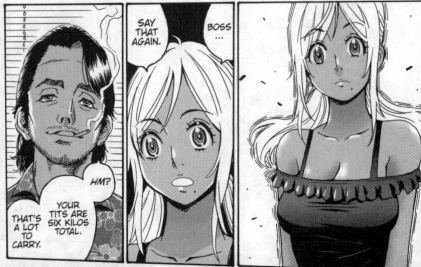

SAY THAT AGAIN.

BOSS...

HM?

THAT'S A LOT TO CARRY.

YOUR TITS ARE SIX KILOS TOTAL.

FAST! HEY, IT'S THE BOOB GODDESS. AH.

I'VE NEVER BEEN SO COMFORTABLE...

THIS IS GREAT!

TUP TUP TUP TUP

スタスタ

IF YOU LOOK AT HER, YOU'RE CURSED TO SUCK AT KARAOKE.

SCARY STUFF.

TAP TAP TAP

DON'T!

HUH? WHY NOT?

SMACK

LET'S PRAY!

FOR BOOBS!

SHE SANG ON A LATE-NIGHT SHOW. IT WAS GIAN-LEVEL BAD.*

I SAW IT ON YOUTUBE.

THE BOOB GODDESS IS A TV PERSONALITY.

CRIMSON RED / END

*The bully character in Doraemon, known for his terrible singing.

Shizuka na yoru ni, by Tanaka Rie from Gundam Seed DESTINY

ANTEATER ESCAPES
アリクイ逃げる

A TRUCK BOUND FOR THE UENO ZOO HAS ROLLED OVER ON THE HIGHWAY...

LEADING TO THE ESCAPE OF A LARGE ANTEATER.

PHWEE!

THEY SHOULD JUST EAT SOMETHING BIGGER.

IT SAYS THEY EAT THIRTY THOUSAND ANTS A DAY.

YEAH, DUDE!

HOT!

BIO I

AH!

URK! CLASS REP!

FWUMP

BOYS ARE SO GROSS!

WHAT'RE YOU LOOKING AT?

LET'S DO OUR BEST, TOO!

THE BOOB GODDESS IS A STAR!

NOT SURE.

AT WHAT?

LY COMIC MAGAZINE

YOUNG

8/25

340 YEN

HEAVEN

NO BOOBS... NO JUSTICE!

4PGS COVER GRAVURE HAEBARU ISORA

SERIOUSLY...?

WANNA CATCH AN ANT-EATER?

SO...

GLOBE-TROTTING BEAST WRANGLERS
PRODUCER
Narumi Shuranosuke

MY KARATE?!

THIS CALLS FOR SPECIALISTS-- THE POLICE, OR THE MILITARY!

YOU SHOULD TAKE IT DOWN... WITH YOUR AMAZING KARATE!!

IT'S INJURED THREE PEOPLE-- AND IT'S STILL AT LARGE.

IT'S BEEN A WEEK SINCE THE ACCIDENT.

I THINK...

BORING, HUH?

YEAH...

IT'S NOT COMING.

YEAH...

3:00 A.M.

I'VE NOTICED.

WELL, IT AIN'T ALL BAD...

I'VE BEEN ENJOYING THE SCENERY.

I'M AN ASSISTANT DIRECTOR!

HEH HEH!

YOU KNOW...

I'M USED TO IT.

IT'S JUST LOOKING.

STOP ANYTIME.

YOU DID?

IS THAT OKAY?

DON'T PLAY FRIGID, WHORE.

WHAT?

TSK!

I'M AN IDOL, NOT...

YOU KNOW!

SMUSH

WHAT'S THE BIG DEAL?

YOU'RE A GRAVURE IDOL.

LET'S GET ACQUAINTED...

OKAY?

POP

IS IT THAT I'M JUST A LOSER ASSISTANT DIRECTOR?

YOU LET YOUNG PUNKS AND SUGAR DADDIES COP FEELS.

GO AHEAD.

I'LL TELL NARUMI!

I--

STOP.

HM?

LET'S WORK TOGETHER.

HUH?

FLICK
FLICK
FLICK
FLICK
FLICK

NOT THERE!

NO...

THAT'S NOT HONEY!

STOP THAT...

SMACK

SMUCK

SUCK

SLUCK

SHLUCK

WAIT, WAIT!

NO WAY!

SLURP
SLURP
SLURP
SLURP

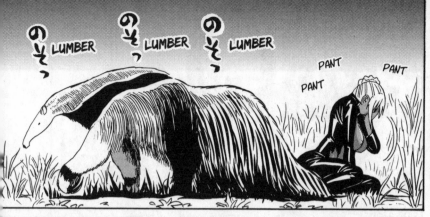

LUMBER LUMBER LUMBER

PANT PANT PANT

OFF TO THE ZOO WITH YOU!

HEH

I CAUGHT YOU!

GRAB

GLARE

THERE IS NO VICTOR OR LOSER.

IF ONE BEFRIENDS AN ENEMY...

YEEK!

LICK

YOU'RE BEING GOOD!

HUH?

SNAKES, TOO?!

大蛇も！？

AS FOR THE ZOO TRUCK ACCIDENT...

THE ANTEATER WAS NOT THE ONLY ESCAPED ANIMAL. AN EIGHT-METER-LONG ANACONDA IS ALSO ON THE LOOSE!

THE POLICE ARE CURRENTLY LOOKING INTO TRANSPORT COMPANIES...

SLITHER

SLITHER

GOOD LITTLE ANTEATER!

ON A QUIET NIGHT / END

Booty
Royale

Never
Go Down
Without a
Fight!

CHAPTER 6 | WHISPER OF A FLOWER

Hana no Sasayaki is the name of the OP to the 1985 anime adaptation of the novel A Little Princess

The Erotic Iron Woman

Goujima Sara

〒 160-0023
東京都新宿区西新宿 6-69-9-1413
090-4481-8366
sara_doj/ima@ybb_ne_jp

LET'S GO GET DRUNK, OKAY?

CALL ME.

I LIVE IN THE NEIGHBOR-HOOD.

WE'LL FIGURE IT OUT.

NO DRINKS FOR ME.

I'M A MINOR THOUGH...*

The Erotic Iron Woman
Goujima Sara

*Drinking age in Japan is twenty. The legal age for AV performers is eighteen.

COLD

SEE YOU LATER!

I'LL BE WAITING!

OKAY!

HURRY UP.

SHE SEEMS SO DOWN-TO-EARTH.

HUH... HAEBARU

PEEP

THE GIANT ANTEATER KILLED THE ANACONDA. IT SAVED ME...

SLICE

DAMAGE!

SLIDE

THE STOMACH ACID RUINED MY HAIR, SO I CUT IT...

KARATE IS FOR HUMAN OPPONENTS!

I WAS ARRO-GANT...

?

SOB SOB

SOB

SHH...

COME ON!

NATU-UURE!

I WAS SHO FOOLISH!

WAHHH!

WHIINE

THE NEIGH-BORS...

WHAT A LIGHT-WEIGHT.

I LOSHT...!

IN THE END...

AGAINSHT A WILD ANIMAL...

THE EROTIC

I'M IN MY THIRD YEAR, AND I'VE STARRED IN FIVE HUNDRED.

HEH, YES.

IRON WOMAN

SO, THE DVDs...

THEY'RE ALL YOUR WORK?

ズラズラ

I'M THE REAL DEAL...

NOT SOME IDOL IN A SWIMSUIT!

AMAZING, HUH?

THASH AMAZING!

YOU'RE ONLY A YEAR OLDER THAN ME.

WOW...

SARA-SAN...

SHALL WE FIGHT AGAIN?!

I WON'T LOSE THIS TIME.

SHIFT

A CHAL-LENGE?!

OHH?

MURG...

UNFORTUNATELY FOR ME, HE WAS A TRUE LOLICON.

RELAX, I MEANT MY **STEP-**FATHER.

MY MOTHER REMARRIED TEN YEARS AGO.

THAT FUCKING SUCKED!

LIKE, ARE YOU FUCKING SHITTING ME?

MY MOM PRETENDED SHE DIDN'T SEE. WHAT A BITCH!

IT WAS EVERY AFTERNOON...

UH...

AH...

I'M SORRY...

UM...

EVERY SINGLE DAY...

ALL I COULD THINK WAS... I DIDN'T WANT TO GO HOME.

YOU CAN'T PLUG YOUR EARS NOW!

INDIFFERENCE IS THE GREATEST EVIL!

EH, IT'S IN THE PAST!

COIL

WAHHH, I'M SORRY!

WHEN I ENTERED MIDDLE SCHOOL, I SEDUCED THE SCARIEST SENPAI IN TOWN...

AND GOT HIM TO BEAT THE SHIT OUT OF MY DAD.

BESSATU GORAKU

*Bessatu Goraku is the name of the magazine in which this manga was serialized.

I THINK I'VE HEARD ENOUGH!

MORE THAN ENOUGH!

WHATCHA THINK, OKINAWA GIRL?

AFTER THAT, I WAS THE CUM DUMPSTER OF THE BIGGEST MOTORCYCLE GANG IN GUNMA PREFECTURE.

IT'S SEX, DRUGS, AND ROCK AND ROLL.

I LEFT EVERYTHING BEHIND IN GUNMA.

MY WORTHLESS PAST BELONGS TO AKIKO.

SARA ISN'T MY REAL NAME.

HUH?

KOJIMA AKIKO.

SARA-SAN...

SNIFF

Y-YOU'VE BEEN THROUGH A LOT, HUH...

WAIT, DO I HAVE WORK TODAY...?

OH, THANKS...

SO I'M HEADING OUT.

STAY AS LONG AS YOU LIKE.

I'VE GOT CLASS...

THROB THROB THROB

WHAT WAS IT?

URK, MY HEAD HURTS...

THIS, WHEN SHE'S GOT A HANG-OVER...?

I STILL WANT HER...

LONE WOMAN OF THE GROUP, HAEBARU MISORA!

WOOO...

AND IT'S OUR SPECIAL COMPETITOR WHO WINS IT ALL...

I GOT IT!

THE BEACH FLAG GAME IS OVER!

PUMP

WHOA!

4

5

6

WHISPER OF A FLOWER / END

CHAPTER 7 | ACTIVE HEART

*Active Heart is the OP for Gunbuster, sung by Noriko Sakai

BEING INSIDE THAT SNAKE'S STOMACH MELTED MY HAIR... YOU GUYS HAVE TO WATCH OUT!

ANTEATERS ARE INCREDIBLE!

THEIR CLAWS ARE POWERFUL.

WHOOPS! LOOKS LIKE A GUEST HAS AN ANNOUNCEMENT! KAKE-RUUU!

WELL, THAT'S IT FOR STORYTIME THIS WEEK!

YEEK! MY AGENCY WOULDN'T ALLOW IT!

SO BERUKO, WANNA TRY GETTIN' ATE BY AN ANACONDA? THAT ANACONDA WANTED SOME!

MY NEW FILM WHAT'S WRONG WITH BEING A TROPICAL FISH? OPENS THIS WEEKEND!

YES!

SEE Y'ALL NEXT WEEK!

I DO MY OWN STUNTS, EVEN THE SWORD FIGHTING SCENES. I'M EXCITED, SO I'D LOVE IT IF--

TV STUDIO BIGWIGS.

HA HA!

THE ONES WHO BACK MAJOR PRODUCTION HOUSES...

CHAIRMEN OF MAJOR ORGANIZATIONS, YOUNG GUYS ON THE MAKE, CHINESE MILLIONAIRES.

SPONSORS. CEOs.

LIKE YOU AND ME.

OF COURSE, EVERY AGENCY WILL SEND IN THEIR POPULAR TALENT AS HOSTS AND HOSTESSES.

OHHH...

I HAD NO CLUE.

BASICALLY, IT'S SOCIAL EVENT FOR VIPs.

AND SO ON.

SUUUURP

ACTORS, MODELS, AND IDOLS ALL WANT PATRONS...

AND RICH MEN WANT TO OWN SOME TALENT. MAYBE FIND A MISTRESS.

IT WORKS OUT.

HEEEY, BERUKO-CHAN!

OVER HERE, OVER HERE!

COMING!

AH, OKAY.

I KNOW WHAT THE BOSS MEANT NOW.

SO I'VE GOT TO CATCH MYSELF A GREAT ADULT.

I WANT TO START SAVING WHILE I'M STILL YOUNG...

SEE YOU!

I'VE BEEN SUMMONED.

WHY SHOULD I SMILE AND GET GROPED BY OLD MEN AND WOMEN?

I'M AN ACTOR.

MY MANAGER MADE ME COME, TOO...

BUT I HATE IT.

WHI--RRR

にこ…SMILE

DIING

RIGHT!

RIGHT?

YOU LIVE HERE?

SENO-SAN...

WHAT DO I DO?

HM?

OH, I DON'T LIVE HERE.

HEY... DOES THAT MEAN...

HIS PLACE, ALL OF A SUDDEN?

HUH?

THERE'S AN APART-MENT ON THIS FLOOR.

WANNA DRINK?

WHIRRR

STRAW?

A TEST TUBE?

LIGHTER?

WHAT?

SUUUU

A SPOON...

POWDER...?

FROM THE OWNER OF THIS FLAT.

I GOT IT UP-STAIRS.

OH, THIS?

DON'T WORRY ABOUT IT.

IT'S JUST SOME STUFF.

GA HA...

SWAY

HAH...

TAP

HACK HACK HACK HACK HACK

ONCE YOU'VE COME BACK TO YOUR SENSES, PLEASE HYDRATE.

HACK

SWEAT SWEAT SWEAT

I LEARNED IT FROM MY FATHER-- EMERGENCY FIRST-AID FOR OLD DRUNKS.

I HIT PRESSURE POINTS TO INDUCE SWEATING AND URINATION...

THUD

GOOD- BYE.

AFTERWORD

I'VE BEEN A MANGAKA FOR JUST OVER A DECADE. I'VE NEVER FELT THE NEED TO STICK TO A GENRE, SO I'VE DRAWN LOTS OF THINGS: A STORY ABOUT MARTIAL ARTS, A STORY ABOUT MONSTERS AND HEROES, A STORY ABOUT GODS AND SAME-SEX LOVE, A STORY ABOUT DEMONS AND HUMANS, A STORY ABOUT POLITICIANS AND ELECTIONS, A STORY ABOUT HISTORY AND WITCHES, A STORY ABOUT JIAN ZHEN COMING TO JAPAN, A STORY ABOUT A DOCTOR, A STORY ABOUT A VOICE ACTOR...

THIS TIME, IT'S A MANGA ABOUT IDOLS.

I DON'T MEAN THE SORT OF IDOLS WHERE THERE'S DOZENS OF THEM AND THEY SELL CRAZY NUMBERS OF CDs AND YOU CAST VOTES, OR THE SORT WHO ARE ALL COLOR-CODED LIKE SENTAI HEROES. THOSE SORTS OF IDOLS SEEM LIKE A SPORTS TEAM, AND I DON'T REALLY GET IT. THIS IS A STORY ABOUT THE GRAVURE IDOL OF DAYS GONE BY, FIGHTING ALL ALONE WITH ONLY HER HANDS. WELL, AND HER BIG BOOBS AND SEXY CLOTHES.

THAT SORT OF IDOL WAS SEEN AS FAP MATERIAL. SHE WOULDN'T EXPECT TO BE POPULAR WITH WOMEN. MOST OF HER FANS JUST WANT HER TO GO INTO PORN AND SHOW IT ALL. IF YOU THINK ABOUT IT, THE PURPOSE OF AN IDOL IS TO VISIT THE DARK, NASTY BEDROOMS OF ALL US LONELY AND HOPELESS MEN—BEING WITH US THROUGH PHOTOS OR DVDs. THEY'RE COMPANY ON THE JOURNEY THROUGH OUR FILTHY FANTASIES.

CAREFREE TYPES WHO'LL SPOUT THINGS LIKE "I'M CHEERING HER ON" OR "SHE GIVES ME STRENGTH"—WELL, THAT'S FINE FOR WHAT IT IS. YOU CAN BELIEVE IN A GRAVURE MODEL OR NOT, IT DOESN'T MATTER. WHAT MATTERS IS IF SHE COMES WITH YOU IN THE DARK.

WHAT WAS I TALKING ABOUT AGAIN? WHO CARES WHEN THERE'S DARK SKIN AND BOOBS. THAT'S WHY I'VE DRAWN THESE MOMENTS IN THE LONG LIFE OF FICTIONAL AV AND TV STAR, HAEBARU MISORA. I HOPE YOU ENJOY IT, AND THAT YOU'RE CHEERING HER ON WHILE HOPING SHE JUST GOES INTO PORN.

FRANKLY, I HOPE SHE DOES, TOO.

—THE AUTHOR

02

Booty Royale

Never
Go Down
Without a
Fight!

CONTENTS

CHAPTER 8 | VIVA! GIRLS' ALLIANCE

FRANK-LY... I THOUGHT YOU'D FLOP.

HARA AKIRA'S MANAGER. ONCE AGAIN IS HER AGENCY.

SHE'S THE ONE WHO CAME UP WITH THIS PROJECT.

THIS WAS HER IDEA.

I GUESS IN SHOWBIZ, THREE C-LISTERS ADD UP TO AN A...

AND WE'RE DEBUTING AS A SINGING GROUP!

YEAH!

BUT WE'RE COMING OUT AHEAD.

GLAD I WAS WRONG.

THEY SAY...

I'M NOT SURE.

NOTH-ING'S MORE EXPEN-SIVE THAN FREE.

YOU'RE THE COMIC RELIEF...

WOO.

MY DREAM OF POP STARDOM IS WITHIN REACH!

BIG SCOOP!

K-CUPS IN HOT WATER!
A FORBIDDEN YURI LOVE?!
Total bust circumference: Over 2m!!

Haebaru Misora sings in the key of G-cup!
...photos of the K&G of KGB...re worth
...d words—and they're a...ship
...discovered on the tenth of
...rs saw them ya...

TOO KINKY!

THINK IT FEELS GOOD? WITH A GIRL?

HUH.

THE BOOB GODDESS LIKES GIRLS!

IMAGINE IT.

YEAH, BUT...

NAW, IT'S QUEER-BAIT.

FAKE NEWS!

FOR REAL?

LES-BIANS, EH?

AKIRA AND MISORA.

NEVER TOUCHED BY THE HANDS OF MEN...

TEE HEE!

FOUR HUGE BOOBS...

UNDER THAT POOF.

YOU'RE A POET...

YEP.

HEH!

I CHOOSE TO BELIEVE THERE IS BEAUTY IN THIS WORLD.

THE BROKEN-HEARTED SARA-SAMA AT A ROPPONGI DALE-STRIBE ORGY!

WHYYY?!

BOINK BOINK BOINK

WHY HER AND NOT ME?!

SHE'S INSATIABLE...

MISO-RAMEN!

WAHHHHHH!

LISTEN UP!

THIS IS THE WARRING STATES PERIOD OF IDOLDOM!

IT'S NOT ENOUGH TO BE SEXY!

YOU HAVE TO SURPRISE THEM!

LIKE IT OR NOT, YOU'RE LESBIANS NOW!

DON'T SLIP UP!

JAB

BAM

YES'M!

I'VE GOT SOMETHING ELSE FOR YOU.

WHAT ABOUT ME?

STAND...

[SOB] I... UNDER...

PANT

PANT

PANT

LET'S DO OUR BEST!

MIZUTANI YUKI!...

FEARSOME GIRLBOSS MANAGER!

CLICK

CLICK

CLICK

SURE IS TOUGH.

WORKING IN A GROUP...

LONG TIME NO SEE.

HIYA, SWEETHEART.

WHIIIR

President Ootomo Kikuichi
OF OFFICE OOTOMO

WHO WOULDA THOUGHT YOU'D BE GIVIN' US A RUN FOR OUR MONEY.

I'M DAMN IMPRESSED.

BUSINESS SURE IS BOOMING FOR YOU, HUH?

BOSS ...

!!

BANG

HONK

CLICK

WELL, THANKS ...

VIVA! GIRLS' ALLIANCE / END

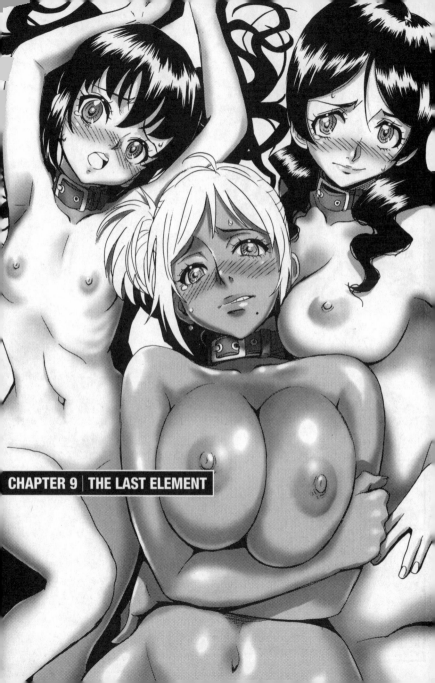

CHAPTER 9 | THE LAST ELEMENT

HNN!

HNOH!

OHH!

ZLUP

ZLUP ZLUP

WHY AM I HERE?!

SOB ...

YUKI-CHAN!

YU...

OR NEXT YOU'LL BE WIPING MY ASS!

DO A GOOD JOB, TEAM JAPAN...

HEE

HEE!

WA HA HA HA HA!

NO! HE'S NOT THE BOSS OF ME!

I'LL DEFEND THE OTHER TWO...

AND YUKI-SAN, TOO!

MMMM!

ARE YOU TV VIRGINS READY TO BECOME DIRTY WHORES?

HAVING FUN YET, KGB?

WHAT A SPECTACLE!

*FAN: PATRIOTISM IS NO VICE.

AND TONIGHT'S MC!

IT'S BEEN A WHILE, MISO-RAMEN!

WHY?! BECAUSE I'M THE JIZZ GODDESS OF NIPPON...

SARA-SAN!

HEY!

WHY ARE YOU HERE?!

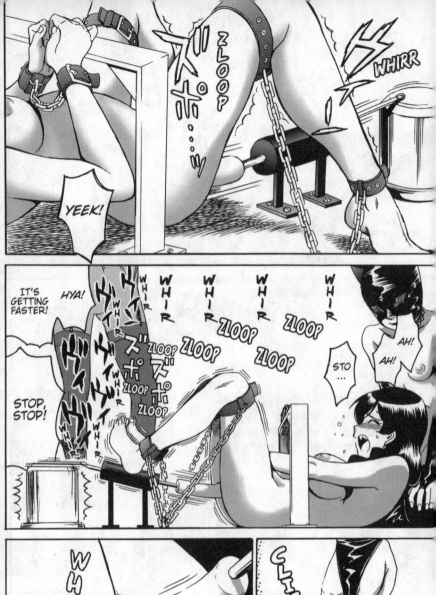

BUT YOU'RE GOING TOO SLOW!

WOW, FIVE WHOLE REPS!

WHOAA!

CLICK

DO BETTER!

LET'S GO!

DON'T GIVE UP, DON'T GIVE UP!

SENPAI'S JUST LIKE SHUU-ZOU...*

*Shuuzou Matsuoka is a tennis player well-known for motivational speaking.

GSHHH

GSHHH

WHILE JACKING OFF!

NO SLACKING OFF...

FWAH HA HA HA!

EVEN I CAN ONLY HOLD IT FOR THREE SECONDS!

ASK ME HOW I KNOW!

GSHHH

GSHHH

I'M CLENCHING WITH ALL MY MIGHT...

HAAH!

HAAH!

THE MOTOR'S SO POWER-FUL...

HAAH!

BUT IT'S TOO STRONG!

WHIRR

WHIRR

WHIRR

WHIRR

I CAN'T! I'M CUMMING!!

SPEWWWW

BSSHA!!

AH!

AHHHH!

*Edo-period water magic performance.

WELL WELL, THE CUMMING CO-ED!

SQUIRTING BEFORE YOU COMPLETE TEN REPS?

BUT YOU'RE NOT DONE!

SPLSH

SPLSH

SPLSH

*A breaststroke swimmer who won gold medals in the 2004 and 2008 Olympic Games.

CLAP CLAP CLAP

<IS THIS MIZUGEI?>*

BRAVO!

PSSSH

*A B'z song featured on international TV for the 2001 FINA World Aquatics Championships.

<WETTER THAN KITAJIMA!>*

<WORLD WATER SPORTS!>

<ULTRA SOUL!*>♪

THAT'S SHOWBIZ, SARA STYLE!

THIS IS THE REAL COOL JAPAN!*

OR IS IT WTF JAPAN?! HA HA!*

PSSSS

BABABA BABABABA

AHN

AHN!

*"Cool Japan" is the name of the national plan to promote Japanese pop culture/soft power.

WHAT A CUTE EXPRESSION!

BUT YOUR ENEMY ISN'T ME!

AND NOW AT LAST, OUR MAIN EVENT!

FLING

GOUJIMA SARA!

GOU...

TREMBLE

TREMBLE

TREMBLE

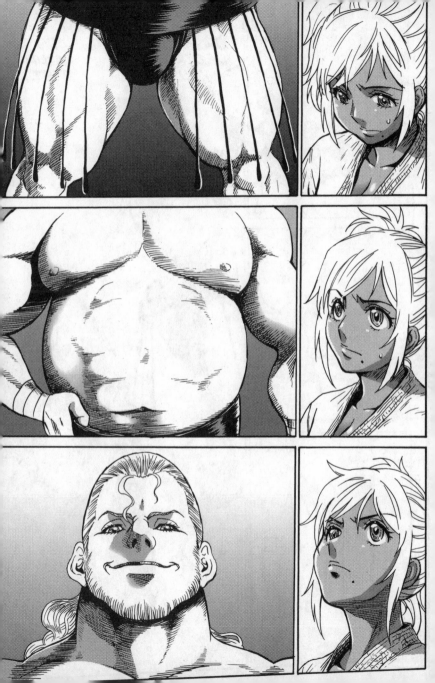

CLEAN, AND DIRTY...

I'VE SEEN A LOT...

SMACK

SMACK

FIGHT!

IT'S BEEN A YEAR SINCE I BECAME A CELEBRITY.

...BUT...

THERE'S NO WAY OUT.

RIGHT NOW, IT FEELS LIKE...

THE ONLY WAY OUT...

SO...

I HAVE THE ONLY WEAPON I NEED.

IS THROUGH!

WAFT...

ARROWS RUN OUT. BLADES CAN BREAK...

BUT AS LONG AS I HAVE LIFE...

I HAVE THIS.

CLENCH

CHAPTER 10 | HERO OF THE RIN

WAA!

THEN A STRIKE WITH THE BALL OF THE FOOT IN A FLYING KICK!

BLADE OF THE FOOT TO THE KNEE. KNUCKLE FIST TO THE SIDE OF THE STOMACH...

<MAGNIFI-CENT!>

<HI-YA! KARATE KICK!>

URK
...

SHE CAN STILL MOVE?!

LET'S
...

SETTLE THIS.

OZEKI!

WOOSH

RAAH

BERUKO-CHAN HAS NEVER CARED FOR MARTIAL ARTS.

RAAH

WITH PLEASURE.

RAAH

COMPETITIVE EATERS HAVE BIG FOOD BILLS TO PAY, YOU KNOW!

BE MY SPONSOR!

YOU'RE A EUROPEAN ARISTOCRAT?

SO, GRAMPS...

HERO OF THE RING / END

CHAPTER 11 │ YOU'RE LIKE ME

CRACK

SKSHHH

OZEKI...

I'M SORRY!!!

SWOO

WITHOUT ANY FUCK, YOU FEEL LIKE YOU GO MAD...

YOU LIKE BEAST, BODY HOT ALL DAY. TOO MUCH TO HANDLE.

ONLY VIOLENCE HELPS!

TREMBLE TREMBLE

I...

TREMBLE

WANTED IT... ♥

YOU WANTED THIS, DIDN'T YOU?

BE HONEST.

BADUM

BADUM

BADUM

SEE?

YOU NO HAVE TO HIDE...

GRRRK

THOSE PRES- SURE POINTS BEHIND YOUR EARS!

I WANTED...

AND I GOT THEM.

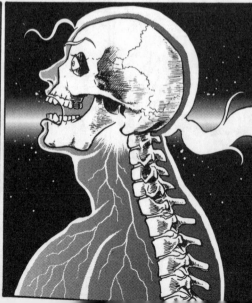

HEY!

AND AUTONOMIC NERVES ARE PARALYZED.

HE'S OKAY. HIS EAR-DRUMS ...

TAKE THIS SERIOU--

GRAB

HEY, OZEKI~!

NO WAY!

I GUESS YOU WON...

SO WE WON'T DO YA.

UNBELIEVABLE!

HEE HEE!

YEAH...

SORRY...

THAT'S FOR BEING ROUGH WITH YUKI-SAN.

THE LONG NIGHT...

FINALLY CAME TO AN END.

BFF!

DO I SEEM SEXUALLY FRUSTRATED?

YEP.

HEY...

LIKE A COW IN HEAT.

BET YOU MOO WHEN YOU CUM.

I DON'T!

YOU'RE LIKE ME / END

Booty
Royale

Never
Go Down
Without a
Fight!

CHAPTER 12 | NAKED MINI

ON THE VERY LAST QUESTION, THE NEW IDOL TEAM LET THE HAWAII TRIP SLIP THROUGH THEIR GRASP!

THAT'S INCORRECT!

HUHH?!

JAN LODENSTEYN

PHILIPP SIEBOLD

ERIK LAXMANN

WILLIAM ADAMS

FRANCIS XAVIER

The names of famous Western historical figures who visited Japan.

WAHHHH!

THE FIRE ARTISTS MEET TOTAL DEFEAT!

VS

ARE THERE NO CELEBS WHO CAN HOPE TO DEFEAT THIS IDOL?!

CELEB TEAM

WINNER!

RYUUKYUU KARATE

NGH...

CEL

HAAH!

HAAH!

PHEW...

ぐったり...

ROLL
ゴロ

YEAH.

TO ASSFUCK NOWHERE IN KODAIRA.

THE TRAINS ARE STILL RUNNING. GO HOME.

THIS OFFICE ISN'T A HOTEL, Y'KNOW.

WHAT'S UP, SUPER-STAR?

NAPPIN' ON THE CLOCK?

SO I'M TOTALLY OKAY...

EVEN IF THE TRAIN STOPS, I CAN JOG HOME...

I'M OKAY.

MY LIFE IS OVER!

SLAM!

I'LL NEVER BE HAPPY AGAIN!

Italian Cafe + Restaurant
SAIZERIYA

MISORA'S NEW DVD?

THIS IS...

KARATE SUMMER

HAEBARU MISORA

HAEBARU MISORA

MEH!

LEND IT TO ME!

FAP-WORTHY?

HOW WAS IT?

PLEASE!

IT'S GAR-BAGE!

GO ON THEN!

IT GOT
BAD
REVIEWS...

YOU
KNOW.

SHOULD-
N'T HAVE
DONE
THAT.

THE DVD
YOU
GAVE
ME.

I
WATCHED
IT.

WHAT
DID?

SARA-
SAN?

SWOOP

HUH?

WHAT
THEY'RE
SAYING
ONLINE?

DO
YOU
KNOW...

BADUM

BADUM

YOU SHOULD LOOK.

EDU-CATE YOUR-SELF.

I DUNNO...

Customer Review
9 reviews
1.2 out of 5 stars
★ ☆ ☆ ☆ ☆

Most useful review
★ ☆ ☆ ☆ ☆
WTF! Why would anyone watch this? She never takes her shirt off and plays in the water in a normal bikini. The extreme nudity and pseudo-sexual moves of her old DVDs are no more. Won't buy the next.

★ ★ ☆ ☆ ☆
False advertisement. The naked apron section in the middle is only maybe okay. Just get naked already.

★ ☆ ☆ ☆ ☆
But where are the tiddies?

☆ ☆ ☆ ☆ ☆
This ain't it, chief. Misora is over.

★ ★ ☆ ☆ ☆
She's specialized for my unique needs: bimbo+tall+huge tits+muscular. I want to be on her side, but I really can't support this sort of fence-sitting. And the boobs she's so proud of looked kinda wilted.

★ ☆ ☆ ☆ ☆
A total ripoff. Give me back my time and money.

Haebaru Misora Karate Summer [DVD]
★ ☆ ☆ ☆ ☆ (9)

About this product
Description
Details
Starring: Haebaru Misora
Sale date: 2015/5/10
Region: Region 2 (This DVD may not be playable in other countries)
Sales agency: Nichibun Shoten
Time: 100 min.
Best seller product ranking
169th – DVD > Idol > female idols

Product description
Content introduction
All shot on Ishigaki Island! The third image DVD from beautiful Okinawan karateka and idol,
Misora-chan! With her ultra-high-impact figure 170cm with a K-cup bust—she bounds boldly under the sun of her hometown!

(From the Cinema Shunpousha Database)

IRONIC.

SHIVER

BUT WHAT DO YOUR **FANS** WANT?

THAT'S WHAT **YOU** WANT...

YOU DON'T HAVE TO DO THAT DIRTY WORK YOU HATE.

NOW THAT YOU'VE HIT IT BIG...

ALL YOUR OLD FANS, WHO BEAT IT TO YOUR EARLY WORK.

YOU'RE FREE TO THROW AWAY...

BUT JUST REMEM- BER...

SNAP

That's it!

Pull it tighter, baby.

Do gre

TUG TUG

BADUM ドク ドク BADUM ドクン

WHAT HAVE I DONE?

I'VE BETRAYED...

MY PRECIOUS FANS!!

BADUM ドクン BADUM ドクン

BADUM ドクン BADUM BADUM ドクン

ドクン ドクン ドクン BADUM

OR GIVING FAKE BLOWJOBS...

OR HIDING MY NIPPLES WITH BUBBLES...

TUGGING ON A G-STRING...

WHAT DO I DO, WHAT DO I DO?!

WHAT DO I DO?

たっ TA たっ TA たっ TA TA

I HAVE A THANK-YOU EVENT TOMORROW.

I'VE GOT TO SLEEP.

I CAN'T LOOK TIRED.

SLSH

I'D FINALLY GOTTEN OUT...

BUT I FORGOT ABOUT THE INTERNET...

IT WAS SO EMBARRASSING.

I THOUGHT...

CHAPTER 13 | PURE GIRL'S TERRITORY

DEAR MOTHER, AND FATHER IN HEAVEN...

ARE YOU DOING WELL?

AND THERE'S A NEW JUNIOR AT MY AGENCY!

IT'S MY SECOND YEAR AS AN IDOL...

WAA!

WAA!

WAA!

WAA!

THERE HAVEN'T BEEN OTHER NEWBIES FOR MORE THAN A YEAR?

PURR PURR

SO THEN BOSS...

SHE'S A TINY HIGH SCHOOL GIRL, ULTRA-CUTE!

SARA-SHINA UTAKO-CHAN.

ALL OF THEM WENT INTO PORN.

BUT...

THERE'S BEEN PLENTY.

POING

POING

OH! WHAT AN HONOR!

AGH, WOW I COULD GROPE THESE FOREVER!

YOU TRYING TO KILL US?! NO MORE SINGING FROM YOU!

MY HEART IS TO-O-OOORN! WHOAAA WHOA WHOA STILLL! GET NO SATISFAC-TION!

PUCCINI. IT'S AN ARIA FROM TURAN-DOT.

WHO SANG THAT ONE?

GORERAI?*

NESSUN?

*Leia is referencing a comedy sketch by the duo 8.6 Second Buskers in which they repeat the nonsense phrase "rassun gorerai."

ANY SONGS YOU'RE GOOD AT?

C'MON, YOU SING TOO, UTAKO-CHAN!

WELL, UM...

DO YOU HAVE NESSUN DORMA?

SO CULTURED!

MA IL MIO MISTERO È CHIU SO IN ME ～～～

LAA

LAA

LAA

LAA

ZKSHHH

WAAAAUGH!

TO THIS DAY, SPECTATORS SAY THE RECORD FOR A DESCENT FROM THE TOP OF MOUNT FUJI WAS BEATEN BY A HUGE-CHESTED IDOL.

WHAT SHOULD I WEAR?

I'M ACTING AS HER MANAGER.

I SHOULD DRESS THE PART.

SLIDE

WOONK

AND WE'LL HEAD TO THE SHO-CHIKUBAI BOOK-STORE IN JINBO-CHO...

IT'S LIKE I'M HER NURSE-MAID!

I'M SUPPOSED TO PICK HER UP AT THREE...

MAYBE A MODEL?

BOOBS NAW. LIKE THAT?

LOOK.

SHE'S ON TV.

MURMUR

SHE IS?

WHOA, WHO'S THAT?

LOOK AT HER BODY!

MURMUR

MURMUR

MURMUR

HOLY HINEMOS SCHOOL FOR GIRLS

CHATTER

CHATTER

SEE YOU!

BYE!

TEE HEE!

GOOD DAY.

BY SUBWAY, I GUESS...

UM...

THEN LET'S GO.

THE STATION IS THIS WAY.

UTAKO-CHAN!

I'VE COME TO PICK YOU UP...

POING

MISORA-SAN!

RMBL

THANK YOU FOR YOUR HELP TODAY.

WELL, SHE DOES LIVE IN THE AREA.

WHO'S IN CHARGE HERE?!

AND SO, THE HIBIYA-LINE SUBWAY CAR NAMED DESIRE...

RMBL

RACES ALONG!

GLANCE

GLANCE

GLANCE

GLANCE

AH... I SEE...

PARDON ME...

MY PARENTS ARE AWAY. THEY WORK FOR THE U.N.

PLEASE, COME IN.

CHAK

LET ME HELP, AT LEAST!

WAIT, NO!

I'LL MAKE YOU SOMETHING.

PLEASE, SIT DOWN AND RELAX.

SCRAPE

APRON

LET ME HELP!

I CAN'T RELAX AT ALL!

OH NO, PLEASE, TAKE IT EASY...

*An Okinawan dish of skin-on pork stewed in soy sauce and brown sugar.

PARDON?

TO MAKE THE WHOLE WORLD HAPPY! ♥

TO USE THESE BREASTS ...

I GOT TEASED SO MUCH. AND WHEN I EXERCISED, THEY JIGGLED ALL OVER THE PLACE.

HMM... FOURTH GRADE?

SCRUB SCRUB

MISORA-SAN, WHEN DID YOUR CHEST START GROWING?

BUT...

A CERTAIN EVENT CHANGED ME.

SAME FOR ME.

PEOPLE LOOKED AT ME DIFFER-ENTLY.

HUH?

IS THAT STRANGE?

UM...

I THINK THAT'S ADMIRABLE...

THAT WITH THE POWER OF MY BREASTS, I WOULD HEAL THE WORLD!

AND SO I SWORE...

SPLOOSH

This has...

opened my eyes, too.

THE NEXT DAY, HIS TESTIMONY...

LED TO THE ARREST OF A BURGLARY RING THAT HAD TERRORIZED THE CITY.

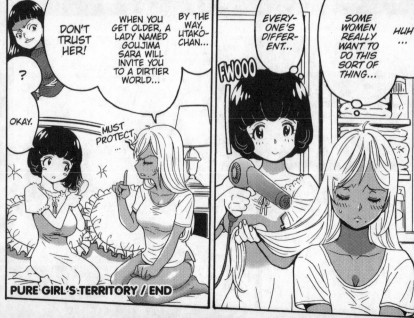

DON'T TRUST HER!

?

OKAY.

WHEN YOU GET OLDER, A LADY NAMED GOUJIMA SARA WILL INVITE YOU TO A DIRTIER WORLD...

BY THE WAY, UTAKO-CHAN...

MUST PROTECT...

EVERYONE'S DIFFERENT...

SOME WOMEN REALLY WANT TO DO THIS SORT OF THING...

HUH...

FWOOO

PURE GIRL'S TERRITORY / END

CHAPTER 14 | GREEN FRUIT

LET'S GO!

ETHNIC SOUNDS GREAT!

THERE'S A NEW INDONESIAN PLACE!

LET'S GO GET A BITE.

THANKS!

THANK YOU.

TODAY IS A KGB SHOOT...

DOING MAGAZINE GRAVURE IN MATCHING UNDER-WEAR.

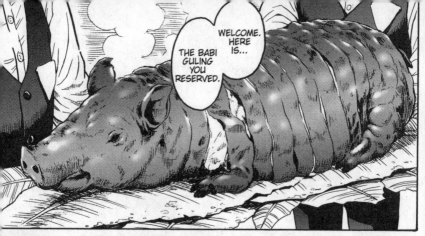

WELCOME.
HERE
IS...

THE BABI
GULING
YOU
RESERVED.

MIE
GORENG.

GREEN
CURRY.

RIGHT
AWAY.

ORDER
YOUR
OWN.

HUH?
THIS
IS ONE
SERVING.

YOU'RE
NOT
SHARING
...?

SLICE

SHOVING
YOUR
PUSSY
AT THE
CAMERA.

YOU'RE
USUALLY
GUTSY...

YOU
WEREN'T
GOING
ALL THE
WAY WITH
YOUR
POSES.

OH, I
DUNNO.

GOBBLE GOBBLE

GOBBLE

GOBBLE

CRUNCH

HUH?
NOT
REALLY.

WHY?

MUNCH
もぐ

MUNCH
もぐ

BY THE
WAY,
MISORA.

WHAT
WAS UP
WITH
TODAY?

FEELING
SICK?

SLICE

NOW THAT YOU MENTION IT...

UM...

RIGHT? SHE WASN'T INTO IT TODAY, WAS SHE?

MUNCH

HOW EMBARRASSING...

SHAPE UP. YOU'RE THE SEXY ONE.

WHATEVER.

MAYBE I WAS A LITTLE TIMID.

TODAY'S MY SECOND DAY.

MAYBE YOU'RE RIGHT...

AKIRA-CHAN.

NO WAY...

ANOTHER PIG!

AHH, MODERATELY FULL!

THAT WAS GOOD!

*Akira-chan is a third-year student at Tokyo University Law.

HUH?

SHOW ME.

SO SHOW ME.

YOU DON'T WANT TO SEE THE DOCTOR.

YOU CAME TO ME, RIGHT?

YOU'RE WORRIED IT'S TOO BIG, RIGHT?

LEAN

LEAVE IT TO ME!

PANT PANT PANT PANT PANT PANT

P-PLEASE...

OH... YEAH!

YOU'RE RIGHT.

THEN...

BUT I CAN COMPARE IT!

I'M NOT A DOCTOR...

STRIP

SLIDE

BADUM BADUM BADUM BADUM BADUM BADUM

SPREAD YOUR LEGS.

I'LL TAKE A LOOK...

I...

OKAY...

I'M JUST SUPER GAY, SORRY!

AH!

WHY'RE YOU STRIPPING TOO, AKIRA-CHAN?

BUT I'M STRIP-PING!

IT IS, HUH?

IS IT BIG?

SO?

SPREAD

IT'S WEIRD?!

URRRRRK!

IT'S STICKING OUT A BIT...

AND THE HOOD... IS PEELED BACK.

WELL...

IT'S TWICE... NO, THREE TIMES AS BIG AS MINE.

AMAZING...

HUH?

HUH

?!

I WANT TO SEE IT EXCITED! THIS IS SCIENCE!

I STILL CAN'T MAKE A JUDGMENT!

DEAL WITH IT!

LICK

YEEP!!

WH-WHA...

PLAY WITH MYSELF MORE THAN OTHER PEOPLE?

IF THE DOCTOR TOLD ME THAT, I'D DIE.

MAYBE I PLAYED WITH IT TOO MUCH...

DO I REALLY ...

SO IT REALLY IS BIG...

WHY?!

UM...

I DOUBT THAT'S RELATED.

......

I DO IT THREE TIMES A DAY.

IT BECOMES ENLARGED BY TESTOS-TERONE.

IN OTHER WORDS, JUST LIKE WITH THE PENIS...

I GUESS ...

THE PENIS.

TO THE MALE ORGAN, RIGHT?

SO, THE CLITORIS IS EQUIV-ALENT...

MAYBE ...

......

MAYBE?!

HAVE YOU BEEN EXERCISING MORE?

LATELY...

AND MORE HORMONES ARE RELEASED AFTER BIG WORKOUTS.

MALE HORMONES STIMULATE THE FORMATION OF MUSCLE AND BONE STRUCTURE...

I-I DUNNO, BUT...

I DON'T THINK MY REGIMEN HAS CHANGED.

I'VE ALWAYS DONE A LOT OF KARATE...

YOU TRAIN ALL THE TIME, HUH?

OH, I SEE.

IT'S THE SAME, RIGHT...?

WHENEVER I HAD A SPARE MOMENT.

BUT I'VE ALWAYS PRACTICED HITTING WALLS AND PILLARS TO MAKE MY FISTS HARDER...

I'VE BEEN BREAKING WOOD AND STONE EVERY DAY FOR WEATHER FREAKS...

WACK

WACK

HAH.

*"signs: "Welcome" (in Chinese)

I'M A MARTIAL ARTIST, FIRST AND FOREMOST...!

UURK... YES...

YOU'VE STARTED DOING IT AGAIN, HUH...

WAK

WAK

THIS IS ME AS I AM!

IT'S FINE!

THAT'S REAL UP TO THE LINE, WHOA.

WHOAA!

HERS IS HUGE!!

DUDE !!

STUDLY !!!

SHE'S GOT MORE THAN JUST BOOBS!!

MISORA'S FANS WERE ACTUALLY OVERJOYED.

SNAP

BOOTY ROYALE 2 / END

AFTERWORD

HELLO. IT'S NICE TO SEE YOU AGAIN.
I THOUGHT YOU MIGHT ENJOY SOME AUTHOR'S NOTES.

CH. 8: VIVA! GIRLS' ALLIANCE
IN CHAPTER 8, THE TOKYO U LAW SCHOOL IDOL HARA AKIRA, WHO MADE
A BRIEF APPEARANCE IN THE LAST VOLUME, SHOWS UP AGAIN. WHILE
SHE PRETENDS TO BE "SHIO-BAITING"—TYPICAL FOR IDOLS THESE
DAYS—SHE ACTUALLY IS A LESBIAN. AKIRA, YUKI AND OOTOMO TRIO
ARE CHARACTERS FROM MY OLD POLITICAL MANGA, ONCE AGAIN!
(SHUEISHA). IN THAT ONE, AKIRA WAS A LAWYER-TURNED-POLITICIAN.
PLEASE GIVE IT A LOOK. THE CHAPTER TITLE THIS TIME WAS FROM THE
ED THEME OF CH. 4 OF SERAPHIM CALL. THE SHOW COMES OFF AS JUST
A DENGEKI G'S-STYLE BISHOJO ANIME, WHILE AT EVERY TURN IT REVEALS
HEAVY SF THINKING—A GREAT SHOW, VERY SUNRISE-LIKE.

CH. 9: THE LAST ELEMENT
EVERYBODY LOVES A VAMPIRE GIMMICK—AND SO WITH MORE SUNRISE
ANIME-STYLE LOGIC, THE HANDSOME SUMO WRESTLER DORAKURYUU
APPEARS. WHEN I CAME UP WITH THE IDEA OF PUTTING THE READING
"CUTE" OVER "SEXUAL EXPLOITATION," I THOUGHT, "I'M A GENIUS!"
THE TITLE IS FROM AN INSERT SONG IN DIGIMON FRONTIER, FROM A
HYPER-SPIRIT EVOLUTION SCENE.

CH. 10: HERO OF THE RING
GETTING INTO THE HABIT OF EXPELLING ALL YOUR BREATH TO
DRAMATICALLY REDUCE BREATHLESSNESS ISN'T ONLY A KARATE THING.
THE CHAPTER TITLE IS FROM RIKISHIMAN'S THEME SONG IN KINNIKUMAN.

CH. 11: YOU'RE LIKE ME
THE TECHNIQUE MISORA USES IN THE OPENING RUSH IS SORT OF
MUAY THAI-LIKE AND TOO FULL-CONTACT. I DIDN'T LIKE THAT, BUT YOU
WOULDN'T EXPECT A MATCH LIKE THIS WITH CONTINUOUS ATTACKS IN
POINT-FIGHTING STYLE ANYWAY, SO I FIGURED, OH WELL. IT'S A
MANGA AFTER ALL. THE CHAPTER TITLE IS FROM THE ED TO MOBILE SUIT
GUNDAM SEED DESTINY. I REALLY LOVE MEER CAMPBELL.

CH. 12: NAKED MIND
WHEN YOU'RE SELLING POPULARITY, YOU HAVE TO THINK ABOUT WHO'S
INVESTING THE MONEY FOR YOU TO MAKE YOUR LIVING. THE CHAPTER
TITLE IS FROM THE OP FOR THE RADIO DRAMA SLAYERS N-EX.

CH. 13: PURE GIRL'S TERRITORY
THE SLAVE LABOR THAT'S KNOWN AS THE "TECHNICAL INTERN TRAINING"
REALLY IS A SERIOUS PROBLEM THAT HAS RECEIVED INTERNATIONAL
CRITICISM. WHEN I SAID TO MY EDITOR SAEKI-SAN TO PICK THIS OR OH
HEART, RETURN TO THE ORIGIN FOR THE CHAPTER TITLE, THEY PICKED
THIS ONE. SERIOUSLY? WHY?

CH. 14: GREEN FRUIT
HERMAPHRODITISM IS THE CLEAREST PROOF OF DIVINITY ON EARTH—
YOU WANT A TRUE GODDESS TO HAVE NOT ONLY BREASTS, BUT ALSO A
LARGE CLITORIS. THE CHAPTER TITLE IS THE OP FOR ULTRAMAN NEXUS.

WELL THEN, LET US MEET AGAIN IN THE NEXT VOLUME.
—THE AUTHOR

SEVEN SEAS ENTERTAINMENT PRESENTS

Booty Royale

by RUI TAKATO   VOLS. 1-2

TRANSLATION
Jennifer Ward

ADAPTATION
The Smut Whisperer

LETTERING
Monica Richards

COVER DESIGN
Hanase Qi

LOGO DESIGN
George Panella

COPY EDITOR
Dawn Davis

EDITOR
Nick Mamatas

PREPRESS TECHNICIAN
Rhiannon Rasmussen-Silverstein

PRODUCTION MANAGER – GHOST SHIP
George Panella

PRODUCTION MANAGER
Lissa Pattillo

MANAGING EDITOR
Julie Davis

ASSOCIATE PUBLISHER
Adam Arnold

PUBLISHER
Jason DeAngelis

READING DIRECTIONS

This book reads from *right to left*,
Japanese style. If this is your first time
reading manga, you start reading from
the top right panel on each page and
take it from there. If you get lost, just
follow the numbered diagram here.
It may seem backwards at first,
but you'll get the hang of it! Have fun!!

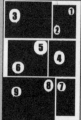

Follow us online: www.SevenSeasEntertainment.com